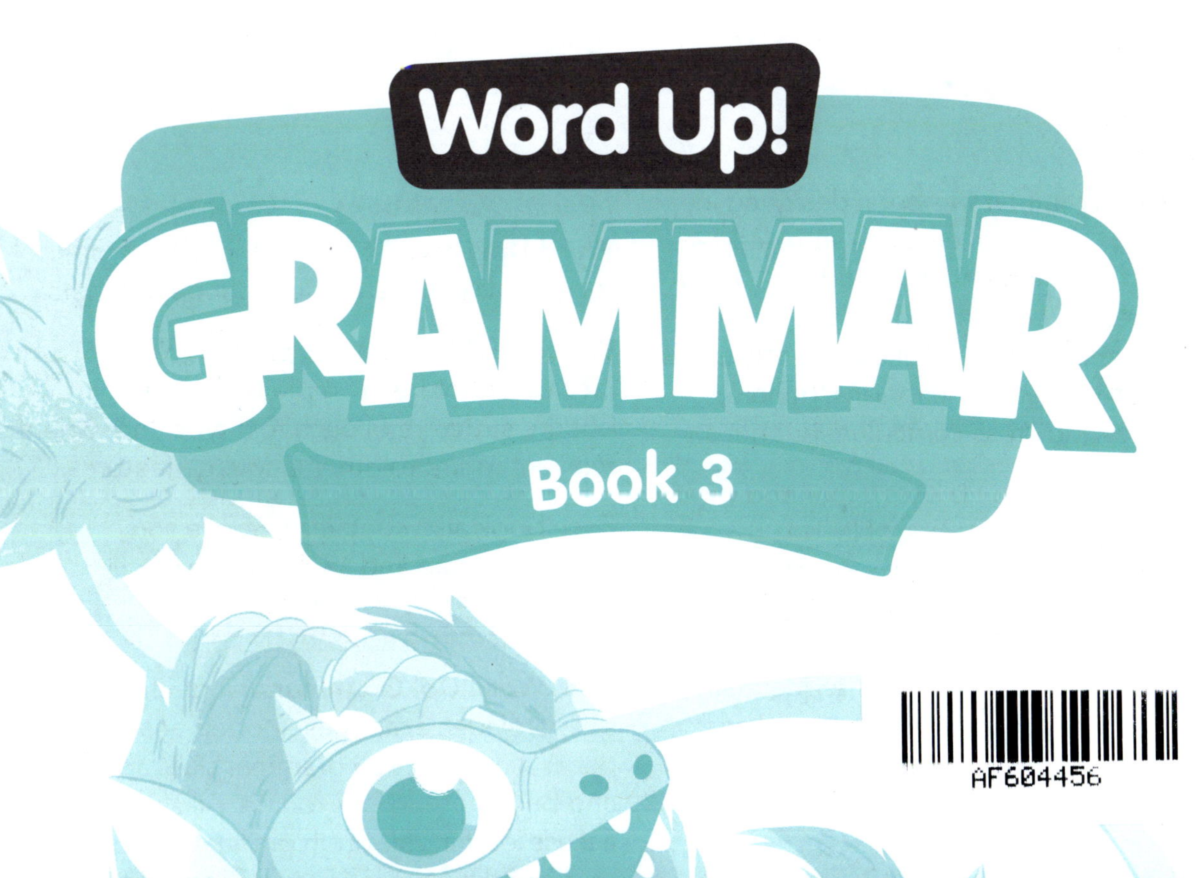

Julienne Laidlaw

Why Do We Need **Word Up!**?

Word Up! Grammar has been designed in response to an identified classroom need – the need for a differentiated student activity book series linked to the national curriculum. Each unit makes explicit links to the Australian Curriculum content descriptions, general capabilities and cross-curriculum priorities.

Grammar knowledge is best expanded when integrated with other areas of language. **Word Up!** promotes listening, speaking, reading and writing through a diverse range of open and closed activities. The series builds on grammar skills sequentially. Each skill is introduced through varied and engaging texts that stimulate critical and imaginative thinking.

What's in it for teachers?

Word Up! Grammar is a flexible and dynamic student activity series anchored by a sound learning scope and sequence. The book demonstrates how grammar features and structures work at a word, sentence and text level. Grammar is practised and assessed through multimodal, traditional and everyday text.

Each book contains 25 four-page units of work. We recommend integrating one unit per week with your current literacy program. Each unit introduces one or two grammar skills in simple language supported by examples.

What's in it for students?

Topics are broad and level-specific. The series engages students by showing them how grammar lives and breathes in their world.

Through the series, students discover figurative speech through colourful lyric poetry, build expressive noun groups in the lost world of folktales and learn the art of persuasion through modal verbs and emotive language.

Series overview

Word Up! Lower (books 1 and 2) has a special focus on visual literacy for younger learners.

Word Up! Middle and Upper (books 3–6) include annotated sample texts that point out the structure of each text type and, where relevant, point to other language features.

Each book also contains a Scope and Sequence map and a Glossary.

Because we're all different ...

Each **Word Up! Grammar** unit defines the skill, provides examples, models answers and paces activities. Key grammar skills are revised and built on from unit to unit. All students access learning through gradually increasing levels of difficulty. The level of support decreases as students progress through learning and practice.

Differentiated student learning is indicated by three icons:

 indicates basic, closed activities with a high level of student support

 indicates a moderate level of student support, with a mix of closed and open activity types

 indicates student-led activities that are writing-centred and open-response

Students can follow the **Word Up!** crazy crab through each unit. When students have completed all units, they receive a Certificate of Completion at the end of the book.

What's in a Unit?

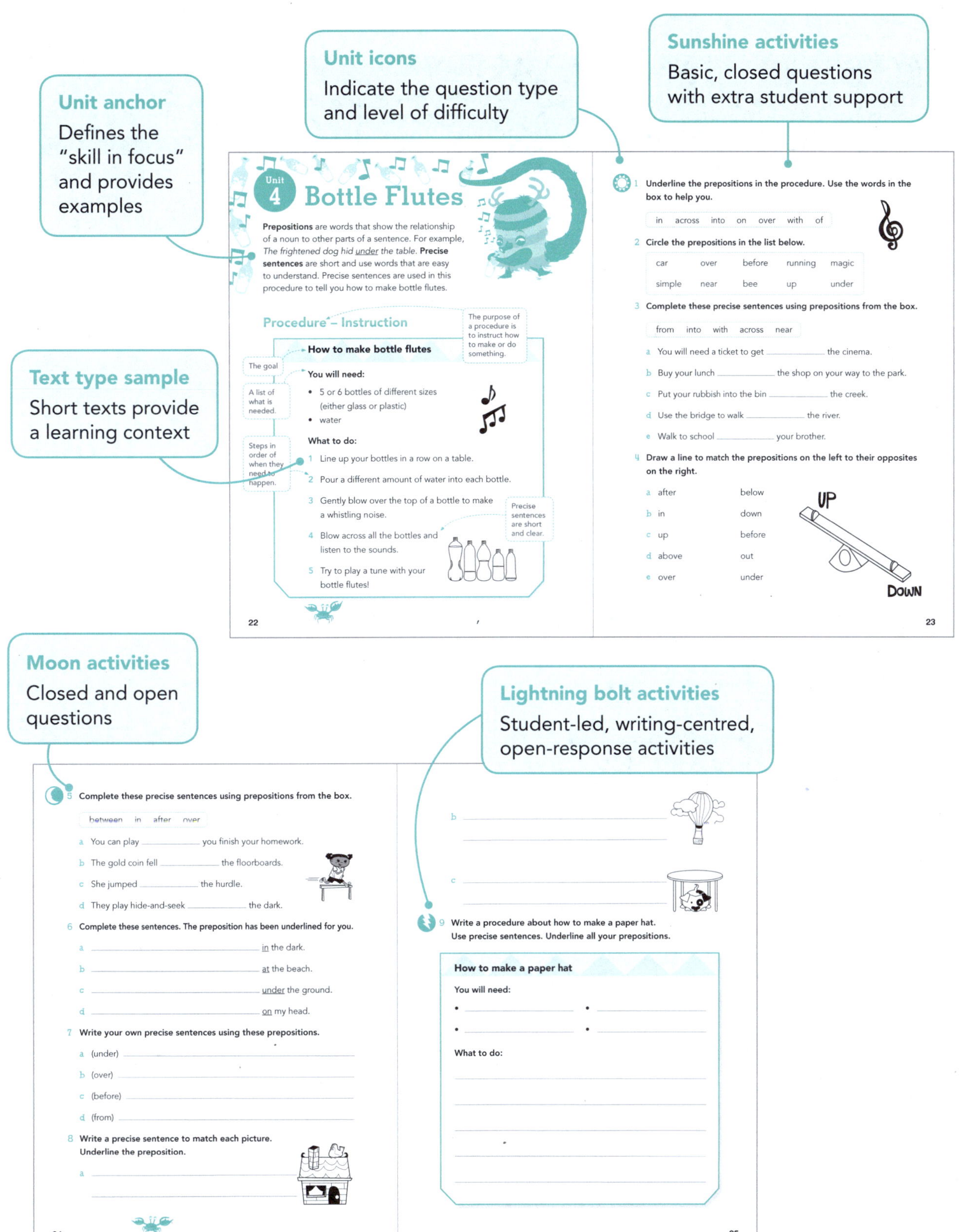

Scope and Sequence

Unit	Unit title	Page	Text / text type	Text and sentence grammar skill	Word level grammar skill	Focus on
1	**Farm Stay**	10	Description: lyric poem	Past tense	Commas	E.g. walked, bought, drove, packed
2	**What Animal Am I?**	14	Description: information report	Simple sentences	Capital letters Full stops	E.g. My baby is called a joey.
3	**An Unusual Visitor**	18	Recount: news report	Factual sentences	Action verbs Saying verbs	E.g. swam, jumped, flew; told, shouted, screamed
4	**Bottle Flutes**	22	Procedure: instruction	Precise sentences	Prepositions	E.g. across, after, beneath, between, over, with
5	**Penguin Life**	26	Persuasive: cartoon	Emotive language	Modal verbs (modal auxiliaries)	Low modality (might, may, could) High modality (will, must, should)
6	**Smoothie Time**	30	Procedure: recipe	Statements of fact	Noun groups Articles	E.g. The tall boy ate an apple.
7	**Teddy Bear Bob**	34	Transactional: personal letter	Expressing opinion	Modal adverbs	E.g. totally, really, definitely
8	**Bank Robbery**	38	Graphic organiser: timeline	Precise language	Modal adjectives	E.g. certain, definite, clear, probable, possible

	Australian Curriculum content descriptions*	General capabilities / cross-curriculum priorities*	Learning areas*
	Understand that verbs represent different processes (doing, thinking, saying, and relating) and that these processes are anchored in time through tense (*ACELA1482*) Also: *ACELT1791, ACELY1683*	• Literacy • Critical and creative thinking	English
	Understand how different types of texts vary in use of language choices, depending on their function and purpose, for example tense, mood, and types of sentences (*ACELA1478*) Also: *ACELA1471, ACELY1682*	• Literacy • Critical and creative thinking • Sustainability • ICT competence	English Science Geography
	Understand that verbs represent different processes (doing, thinking, saying, and relating) and that these processes are anchored in time through tense (*ACELA1482*) Also: *ACELA1478, ACELY1682*	• Literacy • Critical and creative thinking • Numeracy	English Maths
	Understand how different types of texts vary in use of language choices, depending on their function and purpose, for example tense, mood, and types of sentences (*ACELA1478*) Also: *ACELA1471, ACELY1682*	• Numeracy • Critical and creative thinking • Literacy	English
	Learn extended and technical vocabulary and ways of expressing opinion including modal verbs and adverbs (*ACELA1484*) Also: *ACEY1675, ACELY1682*	• Literacy • Critical and creative thinking • Personal and social competence • Sustainability	English Geography
	Understand how different types of texts vary in use of language choices, depending on their function and purpose, for example tense, mood, and types of sentences (*ACELA1478*) Also: *ACELY1682, ACELT1791*	• Literacy • Critical and creative thinking	English
	Learn extended and technical vocabulary and ways of expressing opinion including modal verbs and adverbs (*ACELA1484*) Also: *ACELY1682, ACELT1791*	• Literacy • Critical and creative thinking	English
	Identify the effect on audiences of technique for example layout in timelines (*ACELA1483*) Also: *ACELA1484, ACELA1477*	• Literacy • Critical and creative thinking • Numeracy	English Maths

**Source:* *Australian Curriculum*

Unit	Unit title	Page	Text / text type	Text and sentence grammar skill	Word level grammar skill	Focus on
9	**The Fisher Boy**	42	Narrative: folktale	Compound sentences	Noun groups with adjectives	E.g. The little girl wore a long, blue dress.
10	**Shark!**	46	Recount: personal recount	Paragraphs	Exclamation marks	Identifying a paragraph as a group of sentences about one topic
11	**Term Two Roster**	50	Information report: roster	Repeated information	Technical nouns	E.g. recycle bin, wormery, grey water, compost
12	**All About Me**	54	Description: character description	Clauses	Relating verbs	Identifying a clause as having a noun and a relating verb. E.g. to be, to have
13	**Making Nachos**	58	Procedure: recipe	Commands	Prepositions	E.g. across, after, around, beneath, between, for, onto, over, to, with
14	**Tsunami Wiki**	62	Explanation: wiki	Statements	Subject–verb agreement	E.g. I am happy. We are happy.
15	**Isaac's Interview**	66	Interview: question and answer	Present tense	Apostrophes Contractions	E.g. Isaac's interview E.g. I'll, I've, don't, it's
16	**Izzie's Treasure**	70	Review: film review	Evaluative language	Modal adverbs	E.g. hardly, nearly, clearly, probably
17	**Farewell Party**	74	Transactional: invitation	Phrases	Conjunctions Prepositional phrases	E.g. and, but, for, or, so, yet E.g. over the bridge

	Australian Curriculum content descriptions*	General capabilities / cross-curriculum priorities*	Learning areas*
	Understand how different types of texts vary in use of language choices, depending on their function and purpose, for example tense, mood, and types of sentences (*ACELA1478*) Also: *ACELT1791, ACELY1678*	• Literacy • Critical and creative thinking	English
	Understand that paragraphs are a key organisational feature of written texts (*ACELA1479*) Also: *ACELA1478, ACELY1678*	• Literacy • Critical and creative thinking • Personal and social competence	English
	Identify the audience and purpose of imaginative, informative and persuasive texts (*ACELY1678*) Also: *ACELA1484, ACELY1678*	• Literacy • Critical and creative thinking • Numeracy • Personal and social competence • Ethical behaviour • Sustainability	English Science Maths
	Understand that a clause is a unit of meaning usually containing a subject and a verb and that these need to be in agreement (*ACELA1481*) Also: *ACELA1482, ACELA1478*	• Literacy • Critical and creative thinking • Numeracy	English Maths
	Understand how different types of texts vary in use of language choices, depending on their function and purpose, for example tense, mood, and types of sentences (*ACELA1478*) Also: *ACELA1484, ACELY1678*	• Literacy • Critical and creative thinking • Numeracy	English Maths
	Understand that a clause is a unit of meaning usually containing a subject and a verb and that these need to be in agreement (*ACELA1481*) Also: *ACELA1790, ACELA1478*	• Literacy • Critical and creative thinking • Numeracy • Intercultural understanding • Asia and Australia's engagement with Asia • ICT competence	English Science
	Know that word contractions are a feature of informal language and that apostrophes of contraction are used to signal missing letters (*ACELA1480*) Also: *ACELA1478, ACELY1678*	• Literacy • Critical and creative thinking	English
	Learn extended and technical vocabulary and ways of expressing opinion including modal verbs and adverbs (*ACELA1484*) Also: *ACELA1477, ACELY1675*	• Literacy • Critical and creative thinking • Personal and social competence	English
	Understand how different types of texts vary in use of language choices, depending on their function and purpose, for example tense, mood, and types of sentences (*ACELA1478*) Also: *ACELT1791, ACELY1682*	• Literacy • Critical and creative thinking • Intercultural understanding • ICT competence	English Geography

****Source:*** *Australian Curriculum*

Unit	Unit title	Page	Text / text type	Text and sentence grammar skill	Word level grammar skill	Focus on
18	**The Missing Diary**	78	Narrative: story	Rhythm	Pronouns	E.g. I, you, he, she, it, we, they
19	**Come to Uluru!**	82	Persuasive: brochure	Statements of fact	Modal verbs (modal auxiliaries)	Low modality (might, may, could) High modality (will, must, should)
20	**Bird Life**	86	Description: poem	Rhythmic patterns in poetry	Onomatopoeia	E.g. swoosh, crunch, splosh
21	**Thai Greetings**	90	Recount: postcard	Statements of opinion	Contractions	E.g. didn't, wouldn't, won't, I'm, I've, you'll
22	**Balloon Rockets**	94	Procedure: experiment	Conditional language	Present tense verbs	E.g. What would happen if…
23	**Down by the Sea**	98	Description: song lyrics	Emotive language	Idioms Feeling verbs	E.g. Don't count your chickens before they hatch. E.g. love, hate
24	**The Moon Landing**	102	Recount: historical	Compound sentences	Relating verbs	Parts of the verb "to be" and "to have"
25	**What's a Website?**	106	Explanation: website	Paragraphs	Comparative and superlative adjectives	E.g. strong, stronger, strongest; slow, slower, slowest

	Australian Curriculum content descriptions*	General capabilities / cross-curriculum priorities*	Learning areas*
	Discuss the nature and effects of some language devices used to enhance meaning and shape the reader's reaction, including rhythm and onomatopoeia in poetry and prose (*ACELT1600*) Also: *ACELA1478, ACELY1678*	• Literacy • Critical and creative thinking	English
	Learn extended and technical vocabulary and ways of expressing opinion including modal verbs and adverbs (*ACELA1484*) Also: *ACELA1477, ACELA1478*	• Literacy • Critical and creative thinking • Intercultural understanding • Aboriginal and Torres Strait Islander histories and cultures	English History
	Discuss the nature and effects of some language devices used to enhance meaning and shape the reader's reaction, including rhythm and onomatopoeia in poetry and prose (*ACELT1600*) Also: *ACELT1791, ACELY1682*	• Literacy • Critical and creative thinking	English
	Know that word contractions are a feature of informal language and that apostrophes of contraction are used to signal missing letters (*ACELA1480*) Also: *ACELA1478, ACELY1675*	• Literacy • Critical and creative thinking • Intercultural understanding • Asia and Australia's engagement with Asia	English
	Understand how different types of texts vary in use of language choices, depending on their function and purpose, for example tense, mood, and types of sentences (*ACELA1478*) Also: *ACELY1678, ACELY1682*	• Literacy • Critical and creative thinking	English Science
	Understand that verbs represent different processes (doing, thinking, saying, and relating) and that these processes are anchored in time through tense (*ACELA1482*) Also: *ACELT1600, ACELT1791*	• Literacy • Critical and creative thinking	English
	Understand that verbs represent different processes (doing, thinking, saying, and relating) and that these processes are anchored in time through tense (*ACELA1482*) Also: *ACELA1478, ACELY1678*	• Literacy • Critical and creative thinking • Numeracy	English History Maths
	Understand that paragraphs are a key organisational feature of written texts (*ACELA1479*) Also: *ACELA1790, ACELA1478*	• Literacy • Critical and creative thinking • Numeracy • ICT competence	English Maths

**Source:* *Australian Curriculum*

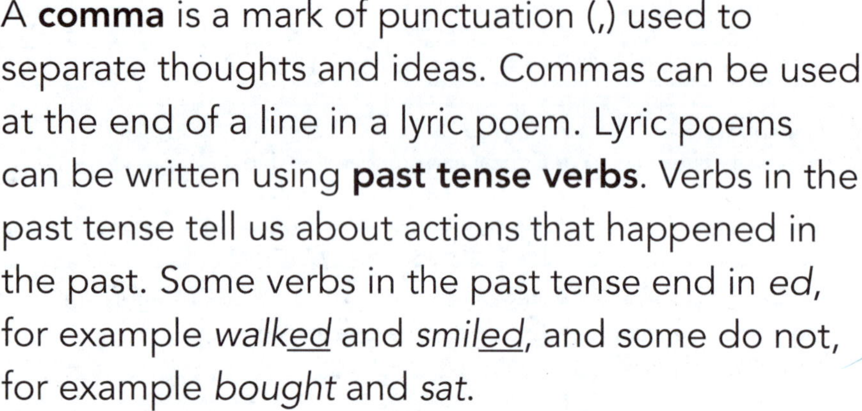

Unit 1 Farm Stay

A **comma** is a mark of punctuation (,) used to separate thoughts and ideas. Commas can be used at the end of a line in a lyric poem. Lyric poems can be written using **past tense verbs**. Verbs in the past tense tell us about actions that happened in the past. Some verbs in the past tense end in *ed*, for example *walked* and *smiled*, and some do not, for example *bought* and *sat*.

Description – Lyric Poem

A lyric poem is a poem that expresses how the writer feels.

The Farm Stay

We packed the car,
And drove for hours,
The city vanished,
Replaced by flowers.

The land stretched out,
The grass was green,
The animals grazed,
The air was clean.

I miss those times,
We packed and went away,
And wish that I,
Was back there to stay.

Commas help us to pause in the right place when reading a poem or story.

There are often commas at the end of a line in a poem to show where to pause.

1 **Circle the commas in the lyric poem.**

2 **Underline the verbs in the lyric poem that end in *ed*.**

3 **Add *ed* to the verbs in these sentences.**

a The wheat crops wav______ in the wind.

b We cook______ our dinner.

c She milk______ the cow.

4 **Change these verbs from the present tense to the past tense by adding *ed*. Rewrite the sentence.**

a pack______

We pack the car.

____

b play______

We play great games.

____

c stretch______

The land stretches out.

____

5 **Add commas to the verse below.**

We milked the cows
And herded sheep
We rode the horses
On hillsides steep.

6 **Write three past tense verbs from the lyric poem that end in *ed*.**

a ________________ b ________________ c ________________

7 **Write three past tense verbs from the lyric poem that do not end in *ed*.**

a ________________ b ________________ c ________________

8 **Complete these sentences using the correct verb from the box.**

climbed watched cooked played laughed

a We ________________ our dinner.

b We ________________ the sun go down.

c I ________________ a great game of chess.

d I ________________ into my bunk bed.

e They ________________ at the clown.

9 **Rewrite a verse of the lyric poem in the present tense. Remember to add commas.**

____

____

____

____

10 **Underline the verbs in your verse above.**

11 **Fill in the missing present or past tense verbs in the table. The first one has been done for you.**

Present tense	Past tense
take	took
	climbed
forget	
sing	
	followed
	raced

12 **Write your own lyric poem about your favourite place and how it makes you feel. Remember to add commas.**

Unit 2 What Animal Am I?

A **simple sentence** is a group of words that contains a subject and a verb. **Capital letters** show the beginning of a simple sentence and **full stops** show the end. Simple sentences provide information in an information report.

Description – Information Report

An information report tells us facts about a topic.

What Animal Am I?

An introduction followed by a series of descriptions.

I am a small marsupial mammal. I live on the east coast of Australia.

I have two thumbs on my front paws. My thumbs help me climb trees. They also help me grip my food. I eat leaves and bark from eucalyptus trees. I have soft, grey, woolly fur. I have a small tail hidden by my fur.

A statement of fact.

My baby is called a joey. A joey is only 2 centimetres long when it is born. It is blind and hairless.

This is a simple sentence.

I can live to be ten years old. I have a great sense of smell. I have excellent balance. I have strong limbs.

I am nocturnal. I sleep in the day and move around at night.

What animal am I?

I am a koala.

1 **Circle the capital letters at the beginning of sentences in the information report in blue.**

2 **Circle the full stops at the end of sentences in the information report in red.**

3 **Underline the name of a country in the information report.**

4 **Circle only the simple sentences below. Remember, simple sentences are short and have a subject and a verb. For example, *The wombat waddles.***

a Crocodiles have scales all over.

b Crocodiles have strong jaws and sharp teeth.

c A koala eats leaves.

d A koala can live up to ten years, but may not live that long.

5 **Add capital letters and full stops to make simple sentences.**

a (koalas) ____oalas live in gum trees

b (they) ____hey eat eucalyptus leaves

c (koalas) ____oalas are not bears

d (they) ____hey hardly ever drink water

6 **Choose two simple sentences from the information report and write them on the lines below.**

____

____

7 **Draw a picture of your favourite animal in the box. Write three simple sentences that describe your favourite animal.**

8 **Put the words in these sentences in the correct order. Remember to use capital letters at the beginning and full stops at the end.**

a sense I smell have great of a

b Australia I on east of live coast the

c have on I my front thumbs paws two

d thumbs climb me my trees help

9 Write two simple sentences that describe what you eat and where you sleep.

10 Write a short information report about an Australian animal. You can choose from the list below. Use the internet to help you.

wombat dingo kangaroo echidna crocodile

Introduction	
Series of descriptions	

Unit 3 An Unusual Visitor

Factual sentences provide information that is true. Factual sentences can contain **action verbs** and **saying verbs**. Action verbs are words that express doing or being. Saying verbs are words used to show speech and are often used instead of the word *said*.

Recount – News Report

A recount tells us about a series of events.

NEWS

An Unusual Visitor

Yesterday, just after lunch, class 3Z had an unusual visitor. Students were busily working on their maths when it entered the classroom without knocking.

The introduction of a recount tells us the when, where and who of the event.

Chloe screamed that she had seen a dragon. Mr Zellio told her not to be silly. Michael shouted when he saw it too.

Paragraphs tell what happened in the correct order.

First, the dragon scurried over to a group of girls. The girls jumped onto their desks in fright. Then, the dragon climbed into the bin to hide. Finally, Mr Zellio took it outside and guided it with a broom towards the garden.

The dragon turned out to be a poor lizard that had taken a wrong turn. The students breathed a sigh of relief and returned to their maths.

News report posted 3:13 pm,
15 March by Drama Girl

1 **Circle the saying verbs in the recount. Use the words in the box to help you.**

told screamed shouted

2 **Underline the words in the recount that tell what the students and Mr Zellio did when they saw the lizard.**

3 **Draw a picture to match these factual sentences.**

a The lizard climbed into the bin.

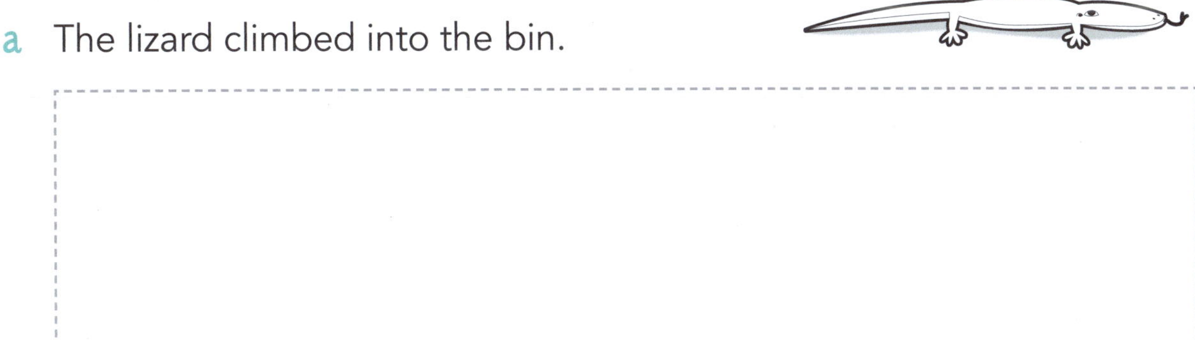

b Mr Zellio guided the lizard with a broom towards the garden.

4 **Complete these sentences using action verbs from the box.**

turned breathed returned entered

a The students ____________ a sigh of relief and ____________ to their maths.

b Yesterday in class 3Z, an unusual visitor ____________ the classroom.

c The dragon ____________ out to be a poor lizard.

 5 **Write a sentence with an action verb to match each picture.**

a ______________________________

____

b ______________________________

____

c ______________________________

____

d ______________________________

____

6 **Rewrite these sentences using different action verbs with similar meanings. The action verbs have been underlined. The first one has been done for you.**

a The dragon <u>scurried</u> over to a group of girls.

The dragon rushed over to a group of girls.

b The girls <u>jumped</u> onto their desks in fright.

____

c The dragon <u>climbed</u> into the bin to hide.

____

d Mr Zellio <u>guided</u> it with a broom towards the garden.

____

7 Write saying verbs in the speech bubbles.

8 Write a short news report about an exciting event that has happened at your school. Circle the action and saying verbs in your recount.

NEWS

Introduction	
Series of events	
Conclusion	

Unit 4 Bottle Flutes

Prepositions are words that show the relationship of a noun to other parts of a sentence. For example, *The frightened dog hid* *<u>under</u>* *the table.* **Precise sentences** are short and use words that are easy to understand. Precise sentences are used in this procedure to tell you how to make bottle flutes.

Procedure – Instruction

The purpose of a procedure is to instruct how to make or do something.

How to make bottle flutes

The goal.

You will need:

A list of what is needed.

- 5 or 6 bottles of different sizes (either glass or plastic)
- water

What to do:

Steps in order of when they need to happen.

1 Line up your bottles in a row on a table.

2 Pour a different amount of water into each bottle.

3 Gently blow over the top of a bottle to make a whistling noise.

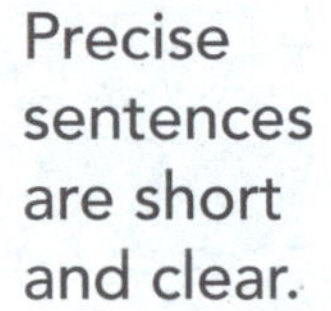

Precise sentences are short and clear.

4 Blow across all the bottles and listen to the sounds.

5 Try to play a tune with your bottle flutes!

1 **Underline the prepositions in the procedure. Use the words in the box to help you.**

in across into on over with of

2 **Circle the prepositions in the list below.**

car	over	before	running	magic
simple	near	bee	up	under

3 **Complete these precise sentences using prepositions from the box.**

from into with across near

a You will need a ticket to get ______________ the cinema.

b Buy your lunch ______________ the shop on your way to the park.

c Put your rubbish into the bin ______________ the creek.

d Use the bridge to walk ______________ the river.

e Walk to school ______________ your brother.

4 **Draw a line to match the prepositions on the left to their opposites on the right.**

a after	below
b in	down
c up	before
d above	out
e over	under

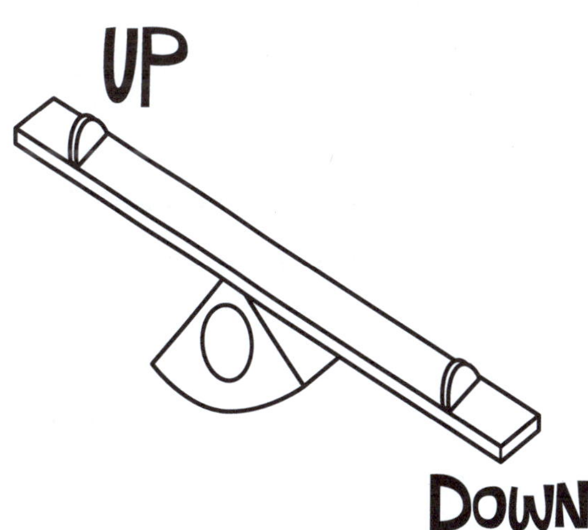

5 **Complete these precise sentences using prepositions from the box.**

between in after over

a You can play ______________ you finish your homework.

b The gold coin fell ______________ the floorboards.

c She jumped ______________ the hurdle.

d They play hide-and-seek ______________ the dark.

6 **Complete these sentences. The preposition has been underlined for you.**

a ____ in the dark.

b ____ at the beach.

c ____ under the ground.

d ____ on my head.

7 **Write your own precise sentences using these prepositions.**

a (under) ____

b (over) ____

c (before) ____

d (from) ____

8 **Write a precise sentence to match each picture.**
Underline the preposition.

a ____

____

b ______________________________

____

c ______________________________

____

9 Write a procedure about how to make a paper hat. Use precise sentences. Underline all your prepositions.

How to make a paper hat

You will need:

- ______________
- ______________
- ______________
- ______________

What to do:

____

____

____

____

____

Unit 5 Penguin Life

Modal verbs are verbs that tell us how likely or necessary something is. Modal verbs may be very likely (*I will go*) or not very likely (*I may go*). Modal verbs are used in this cartoon to help persuade the reader. For example, *I might miss my home*. The cartoon also uses words that make us feel. This is called **emotive language**.

Persuasive – Cartoon

A persuasive text tries to convince you to do or think something.

I am Pat the penguin and I live in the zoo. I meet new people every day and my keeper feeds me juicy fish. I love it here and always will!

Emotive language helps to make the writer's opinion stronger.

My cousin Pete, who lives in the wild, thinks I must be bored in the zoo. He says that I should move to Antarctica.

Opinions *for* and *against*.

Pete thinks I should be diving from icebergs into the great ocean and hunting for my own food.

I could move to Antarctica, but I might miss my home and friends. I would be sad to leave the zoo. I am very happy here. I want to stay forever!

The writer's opinion is repeated at the end.

1 Circle the *should* modal verbs in the cartoon.

2 Underline the *would* and *will* modal verbs in the cartoon.

3 Write a modal verb from the cartoon that starts with *m*.

____

4 Tick the sentences that use emotive language.

a The boxer happily raised his arms in victory.
The boxer won the fight.

b I fell over outside.
I cried in pain as I fell to the hard ground.

c The angry man shouts loudly at the thief.
The man walked past the thief.

5 Find the modal verbs in the word search.

MUST SHOULD WILL COULD MAY MIGHT

E	L	B	M	A	H	Q
N	M	U	A	K	R	T
V	S	H	O	U	L	D
T	D	C	L	J	S	U
G	P	L	M	A	Y	I
O	I	D	L	U	O	C
W	F	T	H	G	I	M

6 **Finish these sentences. The modal verbs have been underlined.**

a You <u>must</u> ______________________________.

b I <u>will</u> ______________________________.

c He <u>should</u> ______________________________.

d We <u>might</u> ______________________________.

7 **Write the missing sentences in the table using low or high modal verbs. The first one has been done for you. Remember, modal verbs can be high in modality (will, must, should) or low in modality (might, may, could).**

Low modal verbs	High modal verbs
I <u>may</u> go for a run in the park.	I must go for a run in the park.
	I <u>must</u> get home soon.
You <u>could</u> wipe your feet.	
I <u>might</u> be on time.	

8 **Complete these sentences using modal verbs from the box.**

might will could should must

a You ______________ work hard if you want to succeed.

b He ______________ be careful when he drives.

c The acrobat ______________ fall if she loses concentration.

d I ______________ starve if I can't find my way out.

e She ______________ be alright if someone helps her.

9 **Circle the emotive language in these sentences.**

a She was disappointed when she didn't win the competition.

b We love to have ice cream after we eat our dinner.

c He is very excited to get a new puppy.

10 **Create your own cartoon using modal verbs to persuade others to clean up Australia.**

11 **Find Antarctica on an online map.**

Unit 6 Smoothie Time

An **article** is a word used to refer to a noun, for example *the man*, *a pen*, *an ant*. A **noun group** is a group of words that builds upon a noun, making the noun more specific. For example, instead of saying, *a boy*, we can say, *a blond boy in a green jacket*. **Statements of fact** can contain noun groups and articles.

Procedure – Recipe

A procedure instructs how to make or do something.

The goal.

How to make a banana smoothie

A list of ingredients.

Ingredients:

- 1 banana
- milk
- vanilla ice cream
- honey

Method:

Numbered steps in the correct order.

1. Ask an adult to help you. Cut the banana into small pieces.
2. Put the sliced banana in a blender.
3. Pour the milk into the blender with the banana.
4. Add a scoop of vanilla ice cream to the blender.
5. Squeeze a bit of runny honey into the blender.
6. Mix the ingredients in the blender until well combined.
7. Pour the smoothie into a tall glass.
8. Serve the delicious smoothie with an apple or a biscuit.

1 **Circle the articles in the recipe. Remember, *the*, *a* and *an* are articles that come before a noun.**

2 **Underline the noun groups in the recipe. The first one has been done for you.**

3 **Circle the correct article in these phrases.**

a a / an university

b a / an man

c a / an shop

d a / an umbrella

4 **Tick the sentences that are statements of fact.**

a Goldfish make the best pets.
Goldfish live in water.

b Snow is very cold.
Playing in the snow is fun.

c Sea World is in Queensland.
I had so much fun at Sea World.

d I think I'll eat some fruit.
Fruit is a healthy snack.

5 **Write the article that goes before these nouns. Choose from *a* or *an*.**

a _____ zebra

b _____ tortoise

c _____ egg

d _____ echidna

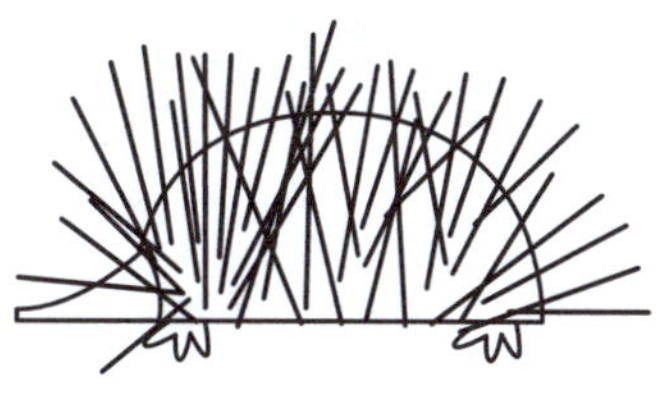

6 **Write a noun group for each noun.**

a giraffe ______________________

b frypan ______________________

c lollypop ______________________

d sand ______________________

7 **Write the correct articles to finish these sentences. Use a capital letter if you need to.**

a _____ gorilla was eating _____ banana.

b _____ aeroplane landed at _____ airport.

c _____ toaster ejected _____ piece of toast.

d _____ elephant had _____ raised trunk.

8 **Rewrite these sentences, adding words that build upon the underlined nouns. The first one has been done for you.**

a The <u>man</u> walked into a <u>shop</u>.

The young man walked into a busy shop.

b The <u>swimming pool</u> was full.

____

c My <u>dad</u> drinks <u>milk</u>.

____

d The <u>bird</u> flew high.

____

9 **Write two sentences describing your school. Include a statement of fact with a noun group.**

____

____

10 **What's in your favourite sandwich? Write your own recipe about how to make it. Underline the articles and noun groups.**

How to make a ____________________ sandwich

Ingredients:

- ____________________
- ____________________
- ____________________
- ____________________

Method:

____

____

____

____

Unit 7 Teddy Bear Bob

Modal adverbs are adverbs that show how certain the writer or speaker is about something. For example, *She is probably the fastest runner in Year 3.* Modal adverbs help the writer or speaker to **express an opinion**.

Transactional – Personal Letter

A personal letter is shared between friends or family.

Personal letters include the sender's address.

23 Bear St
Toytown
Western Australia 5000

Date

8 August

Greeting

Dear Lucy,

I truly miss you. It sounds like you are certainly having a fantastic holiday. You are probably skiing down mountains right now.

I am definitely going with you next time. I am not totally alone at home. I play with the soldiers who march every day across the bedroom floor. The toys next door play really noisy games. Maybe we can join them when you get home.

Yours sincerely,

Teddy Bear Bob

Signature of writer.

1 **Circle the modal adverbs in the letter. Use the words in the box to help you.**

certainly truly definitely totally really maybe probably

2 **Complete the sentences using modal adverbs from Teddy Bear Bob's letter.**

a I ____________ miss you.

b The toys next door play ____________ noisy games.

c You are ____________ skiing down mountains.

3 **Draw a line to match the modal adverb to its correct meaning.**

a maybe	will happen
b definitely	likely to happen
c probably	might happen

4 **Circle the words that could be used to express an opinion.**

a	b	c
I think	She went	You are
I will	She likes	You believe

5 **Choose an adverb from the box to finish these sentences. Draw a picture to match one of your sentences.**

patiently violently swiftly

a The cat waited ____________.

b The bird flew ____________.

c My hand shook ____________.

6 **Choose a modal adverb from the box to finish each sentence.**

truly	really	definitely

a The cat was ______________ patient.

b The bird was ______________ flying swiftly.

c My hand ______________ shook violently.

7 **Write a sentence using each adverb.**

a maybe

____

b very

____

c too

____

8 **Tick the sentences that express an opinion.**

a Canberra is the capital city of Australia.
Canberra is a fun place to visit.

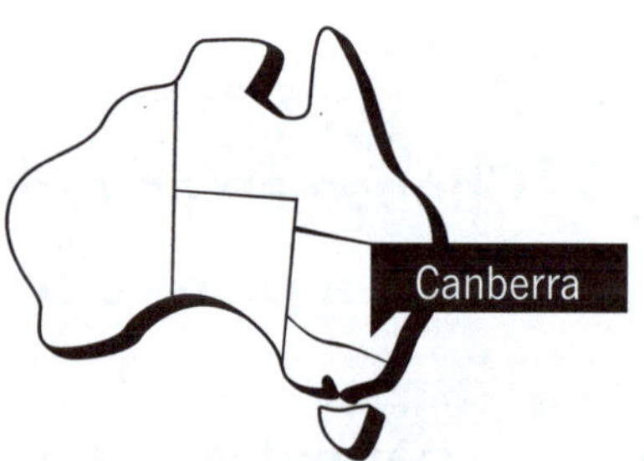

b Soccer is a dangerous sport to play.
There are eleven players on a soccer team.

c Fruit salad is good for you.
Fruit salad is yummy.

d January is the first month of the year.
January is my favourite month of the year.

9 **Underline the modal adverb in the sentence and use it to write a sentence of your own.**

I thought Jai was nine, but actually he's only seven.

____

10 **Write a letter to a friend or family member. Ask them to come to your swimming competition. Remember to include adverbs to help get your opinion across.**

Address ________________________

____

____

Date ___________________________

Dear ___________________________

____

____

____

____

____

____

____

Signature ________________________

Unit 8 Bank Robbery

A **modal adjective** is a type of adjective that tells us how possible or necessary something is. For example, *It is <u>certain</u> I will get a present on my birthday*. Modal adjectives can be used in **precise language** with other words that have a clear and exact meaning.

Graphic Organiser – Timeline

A graphic organiser is a chart or graph that shows information.

The bank manager locks the bank vault at the ACC bank. As usual, he leaves the building after he sets the burglar alarm.

A woman walking her dog nearby hears an explosion. She thinks it is a possible robbery and calls the police.

The police arrive and discover the probable break-in. They break down the back door and enter the bank. They are certain the robbers are still in the building, as they hear voices from the vault.

The police arrest two people wearing ski masks at the scene of the crime. It is clear from the money found in their bags that these are the people who tried to rob the bank.

This timeline shows a list of events in order of when they happened.

1 **The words in the box are examples of modal adjectives. Underline these words in the timeline.**

clear probable possible usual certain

2 **Write four modal adjectives you found in the bank robbery timeline.**

a ______________________ c ______________________

b ______________________ d ______________________

3 **Find the modal adjectives in the word search.**

CLEAR CERTAIN POSSIBLE PROBABLE DEFINITE

E	T	I	N	I	F	E	D
P	O	S	S	I	B	L	E
O	Q	C	P	Z	E	D	U
N	B	M	A	R	F	E	V
E	L	B	A	B	O	R	P
R	T	E	L	K	C	W	Y
S	L	B	A	J	G	X	I
C	E	R	T	A	I	N	H

4 **Write the opposite of these modal adjectives.**

a certain ______________________ c clear ______________________

b unusual ______________________ d possible ______________________

 5 **Underline the modal adjectives in these sentences.**

a It is possible it will rain today.

b Tomorrow there is a definite chance of snow.

c We are certain of sunshine on Monday.

6 **Write the word from the box that best describes how likely you are to do these activities today.**

probable	possible	certain	definite	impossible	improbable

a have a swim ____________________

b have a haircut ____________________

c sleep ____________________

d win the lottery ____________________

e eat lunch ____________________

f fly to the Moon ____________________

7 **Write a sentence using each modal adjective.**

a possible

____

b clear

____

c definite

____

 8 **Write a timeline for your day today and tomorrow. Include some activities that are possible, probable, definite and certain.**

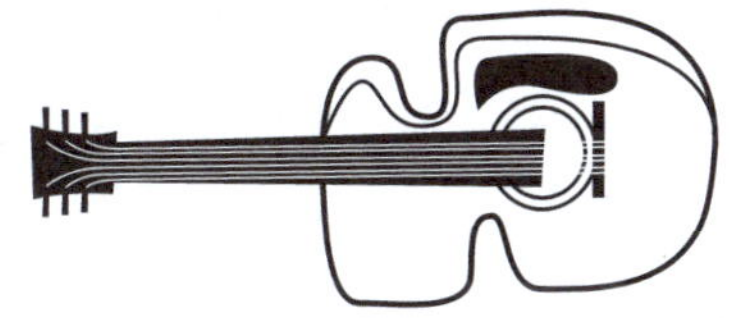

	Today	Tomorrow
8:00 am		
10:00 am		
12:00 pm		
2:00 pm		
4:00 pm		
6:00 pm		
8:00 pm		
10:00 pm		

Unit 9

The Fisher Boy

A **compound sentence** is made up of two simple sentences sometimes joined by a comma. Sentences also contain nouns or **noun groups**. Noun groups are made up of a noun and words that tell us more about the noun. For example, *We ran through the* <u>*dark and gloomy forest*</u>. A noun group can contain **adjectives** that help to describe the noun.

Narrative – Folktale

A folktale is a traditional story, often passed down through generations.

The Fisher Boy

The orientation introduces who, what, when and where.

There once was a small boy who lived with his sick mother by a winding river. Here, the green trees grew tall, and the bright birds sang.

The boy's greatest wish was to catch the most colourful fish in the river. The fish was magical, and people said it brought good luck. The boy and his mother had little money.

Narratives have a problem.

The sequence of events is listed in order.

Each day, the small boy threw in his old fishing line, but sadly caught nothing.

After three days and nights, there was a rough tug on his line. The weary boy had snagged the fish! He pulled it up the muddy banks.

He ran home with his treasure, and his mother jumped for joy.

Narratives end with a resolution to the problem.

1 **Underline the adjectives in the folktale. Use the words in the box to help you.**

bright	colourful	small	tall	muddy	weary	sick	green

2 **Place a tick beside the sentence in each pair that contains a noun group.**

a There was a cottage by the river.
There was a small, charming cottage by the river.

b We ate ten delicious lemon cakes.
We ate cake.

3 **Circle the sentence that is a compound sentence.**

Yesterday we went to the beach, and it was hot.
We went to the beach yesterday.

4 **Rewrite these sentences to make one compound sentence. The first one has been done for you.**

a The bird is small. The bird is blue.

The bird is small and blue.

b The green frog hops. The green frog croaks.

c The girl ran. The girl kicked the ball.

d The man wore a long coat. The man wore a black tie.

5 **Write adjectives to create noun groups.**

a A ________________ dog chased a ________________ cat.

b The ________________ wind whipped around the

________________ forest.

c Suddenly, a ________________ sound came from the

________________ room.

d The ________________ kookaburra sang

________________ from high above.

6 **Join these sentences to make one compound sentence. The first one has been done for you.**

a There once was a small boy. He had wavy, brown hair.

There once was a small boy with wavy, brown hair.

b He lived with his sick mother. He lived by a winding river.

____

____

c His skinny fingers shivered. The poor boy almost gave up.

____

____

7 **Write a compound sentence of your own about where you live.**

____

8 **Write three compound sentences using number and colour adjectives. One has been done for you.**

There were three boys in black jeans.

9 **Write a short narrative using compound sentences and descriptive adjectives.**

Title	
Orientation	
Problem and sequence of events	
Resolution	

Unit 10 Shark!

A **paragraph** is one or more sentences based on the same topic. A paragraph starts on a new line. Writers use new paragraphs when there is a change in topic, a new time or a new place. An **exclamation mark** (!) is a punctuation mark used to give emphasis or show surprise, shock or joy.

Recount – Personal Recount

A personal recount retells a series of events, in the order that they happened. It includes an orientation – who, what, when, where.

Shark!

Yesterday, I went to the beach with my cousins. Yay!

I bodysurfed past the sandbar and caught wave after wave. Suddenly, a loud siren blared. It was the shark alarm!

The lifesavers waved madly and people screamed, "Get out of the water!" I swam quickly to the shore. I looked behind me and thought I saw a fin. To my relief, it disappeared in the waves.

Everyone stood on the shore and was watching the water. The fin appeared again. It was a dolphin!

We sighed with relief, then raced back into the surf.

Each paragraph introduces a new idea.

The recount ends with a personal comment.

1 Circle the exclamation marks in the personal recount.

2 Draw a star next to the beginning of each paragraph in the personal recount.

3 Practise writing exclamation marks in the boxes below.

4 Write four words from the personal recount that have exclamation marks next to them.

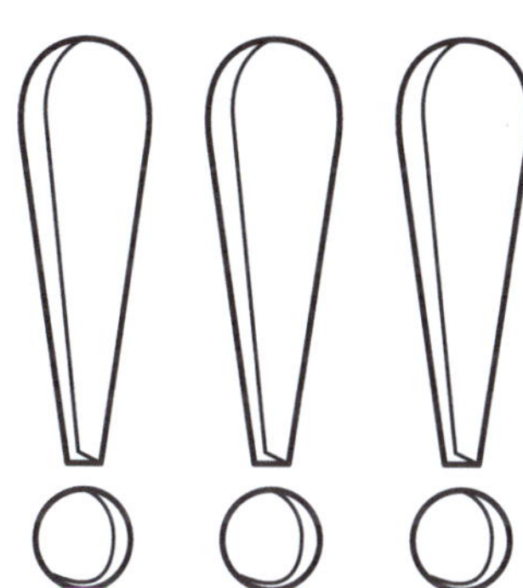

5 Rewrite these sentences, adding exclamation marks at the end.

a Go Australia. You can do it.

b Help. There's a storm coming.

c Happy birthday.

6 **Write a sentence to match each picture. Include an exclamation mark at the end of each sentence.**

a ____

b ____

c ____

7 **Add exclamation marks to the sentences that you think need exclamation marks. Remember, an exclamation mark is used to give emphasis or show surprise, shock or joy.**

a Watch out for the snake

b I am nine years old

c Run, the volcano is erupting

d What a fantastic day

e The monkey ate a banana

f This game is so cool

8 **Draw a line under the word where you think a new paragraph should start. Remember, paragraphs are used in writing when there is a change in topic, a new time or a new place.**

Last week my class went to the art gallery. We travelled by bus into the city to see a special exhibition. We were very excited! At the gallery we saw famous paintings and sculptures. We talked about the paintings. The bus trip home was quiet. Some classmates fell asleep, while others whispered to their friends. We had a fantastic time!

9 Write a personal recount about a scary or exciting time you remember. Include paragraphs and exclamation marks when necessary.

Title	
Orientation	
Events in the correct order	
Ending	

Unit 11 Term Two Roster

A technical noun is a noun used in **technical language**. Technical language uses words that are special to science, art or a particular profession. For example, *A* *<u>thermometer</u>* *is an instrument for measuring temperature.*

Information Report – Roster

A roster is an information report that shows a list of people or groups, their tasks and when they need to complete these tasks.

Year 3D's Green Roster

Title of the roster.

Group	Week 1	Week 2	Week 3	Week 4
Bears	Spread compost	Take waste to wormery	Collect grey water	Put out recycle bin
Tigers	Put out recycle bin	Spread compost	Take waste to wormery	Collect grey water
Cats	Collect grey water	Put out recycle bin	Spread compost	Take waste to wormery
Owls	Take waste to wormery	Collect grey water	Put out recycle bin	Spread compost

List of groups to share the duties.

Tasks are repeated each week.

1 **In which week do the Owls spread the compost?**

____

2 **In which week do the Cats collect the grey water?**

____

3 **Circle these technical nouns in the roster.**

compost   recycle bin   wormery   grey water

4 **Write the duties in the roster that begin with the letters *c* and *t*.**

a ______________________________

b ______________________________

5 **Find these technical nouns in the word search.**

COMPOST   RECYCLE BIN   WORMERY   GREY WATER

S	A	M	W	O	R	M	E	R	Y
O	Q	T	S	O	P	M	O	C	P
K	Y	F	L	V	N	C	M	Q	D
L	R	E	T	A	W	Y	E	R	G
A	R	H	E	Z	L	D	X	K	S
C	G	N	S	U	J	O	I	B	X
R	E	C	Y	C	L	E	B	I	N

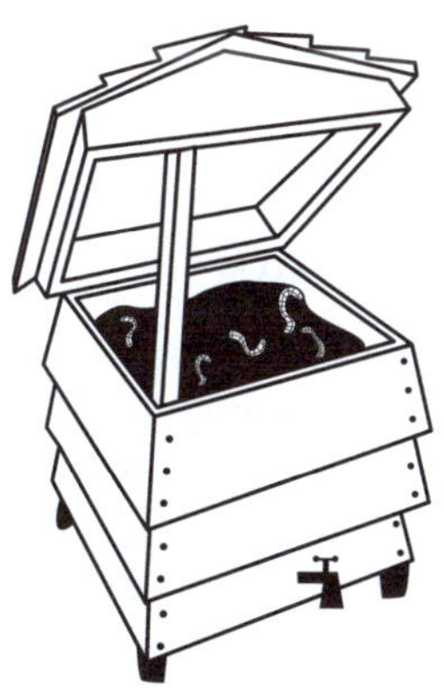

6 **Circle the technical nouns in the box. Write a sentence for each one in the spaces provided.**

ball mousepad rabbit keyboard rocket wormery

a ______________________________

b ______________________________

c ______________________________

d ______________________________

7 **Write a technical noun for each of these topics.**

a Space

____

b Technology

____

c Conservation

____

8 **Draw a line to match the subjects to their related technical nouns.**

a science	software, mouse, internet
b computers	X-ray, syringe, thermometer
c medicine	test tube, experiment, microscope

9 **Complete these sentences using the technical nouns from the box.**

software test tube space

a The astronaut flew the rocket into ______________.

b The scientist poured her solution into

a ______________ ______________.

c I installed the new computer ______________ myself.

10 **Use the roster table to write a roster for some shared tasks in your classroom. Try to include at least three technical nouns you have learned today.**

Group	Week 1	Week 2	Week 3	Week 4

11 **What is your favourite activity from your roster?**

____

Unit 12

All About Me

A **clause** is a group of related words containing a subject and a verb. **Relating verbs** help to show the relationship between ideas in a clause. They can be part of the verb *to be* (*am*, *are*, *is*, *was*, *were*) or *to have* (*have*, *has*, *had*).

Description – Character Description

The purpose of a description is to describe the features of a person or thing.

All About Me

Opening statement / introduction.

My name is Phoenix. I am a ten-year-old boy. I am 134 centimetres tall. I have short, red hair. I have brown eyes and freckles on my nose. I have big feet.

Features and facts about the person.

I am outgoing and my dad has told me I talk too much. I am a friendly person and I try to include others. I love to hang out with my mates.

I can run fast and I am good at kicking a ball. I play the trumpet really well. I like sushi and fruit kebabs.

I love having a good time.

I is the subject in this clause.

1 **Circle the relating verbs in the character description. Use the words in the box to help you.**

am is have has

2 **Underline these nouns in the character description.**

hair boy freckles eyes trumpet feet

3 **Circle the correct relating verb to complete the clauses. The first one has been done for you.**

a I is / (am) a boy.

b I has / have red hair.

c I have / has big feet.

d I am / are good at playing the trumpet.

4 **Complete these clauses using words from the box.**

wore crawled had

a The cute baby ____________________ along the ground.

b The nurse ____________________ a blue shirt.

c The clown ____________________ a red nose and curly, red hair.

5 **Write two clauses describing one of your friends.**

____

____

6 **Draw a line to complete each clause.**

a I ate	the football.
b She kicked	speeding on the road.
c The car was	a packet of nuts.

7 **Write the missing relating verbs to complete the clauses.**

a She ______________ an energetic dog.

b The teacher ______________ explained the answer yesterday.

c The bird ______________ been singing in the tress all morning.

8 **Rewrite each sentence, replacing the incorrect relating verb.**

a I is nine years old.

____

b He is a lovely head of black, curly hair.

____

c Our drama teacher were on stage.

____

d There have a huge spider coming this way. Run now!

____

e Sshh! The baby am asleep.

____

9 **Complete these clauses by adding nouns.**

a ______________________ climbed up the tree.

b ______________________ is a great swimmer.

c ______________________ ran around the oval.

d ______________________ poured out of the pipes.

10 **Write a character description about yourself. Include what you look like, where you live, what you like to do in your spare time, and what makes you special.**

Title	______________________
Opening statement	______________________ ______________________
Features and facts	______________________ ______________________ ______________________ ______________________ ______________________ ______________________ ______________________ ______________________ ______________________

Unit 13 Making Nachos

A **command** is a sentence that tells someone to do something. A **preposition** shows the relationship of a noun to another word. Some sentences include both command verbs and a preposition. For example, *Cook your sausages under a hot grill.*

Procedure – Recipe

A procedure instructs how to make or do something.

How to make nachos

The goal.

Ingredients:

A list of ingredients.

- 1 cup three-bean mix
- 2 cups corn chips
- $\frac{1}{2}$ cup taco sauce
- $\frac{1}{2}$ cup grated mozzarella cheese
- $\frac{1}{2}$ cup chopped avocado
- 2 tablespoons sour cream

Method:

Numbered instructions in the correct order.

1 Ask an adult for help to make this recipe.

2 Put beans in a bowl and mash between the prongs of a fork.

3 Place mashed beans in the centre of an ovenproof dish.

4 Arrange the corn chips around the beans.

5 Pour taco sauce onto the beans.

6 Sprinkle grated mozzarella cheese onto the beans.

7 Bake in an oven for ten minutes.

8 Serve topped with avocado or sour cream.

1 **Underline three prepositions in the recipe. Use the words in the box to help you.**

around between for in onto with

2 **Circle three command verbs in the recipe. Use the words in the box to help you.**

mash bake pour sprinkle arrange ask serve place put

3 **Complete these commands using words from the box. Use a capital letter for each word.**

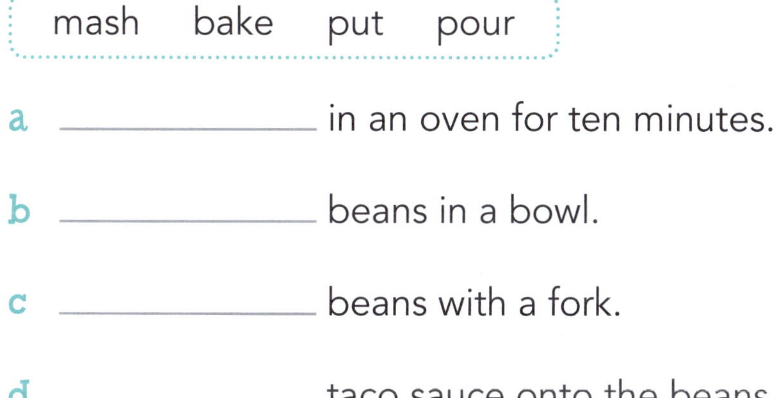

mash bake put pour

a ______________ in an oven for ten minutes.

b ______________ beans in a bowl.

c ______________ beans with a fork.

d ______________ taco sauce onto the beans.

4 **Complete these sentences using prepositions from the box.**

with for around in between

a Bake in an oven ______________ ten minutes.

b Serve topped ______________ avocado or sour cream.

c Put beans ______________ a bowl and mash ______________ the prongs of a fork.

d Arrange the corn chips ______________ the beans.

5 **Complete these sentences using prepositions from the box.**

onto under after across

a You can have dessert __________ you have finished your dinner.

b My uncle's house is __________ the river.

c I found my homework __________ the newspaper.

d The possum jumped __________ the branch.

6 **Replace the underlined incorrect preposition with the correct preposition. Rewrite the sentences using the prepositions you have chosen.**

a Pour taco sauce <u>under</u> the beans.

____

b Bake <u>at</u> ten minutes.

____

c Put the beans <u>beside</u> a bowl.

____

7 **Write three commands using words from the box.**

climb tie pull

____

____

____

8 **Write a recipe explaining how to make a snack of your choice. Remember to include commands and prepositions. Here are some topics you could write about.**

- How to make a chocolate milkshake
- How to make fruit salad
- How to make popcorn

How to make ______________________________

Ingredients:

- ______________________
- ______________________
- ______________________
- ______________________
- ______________________
- ______________________

Method:

____

____

____

____

____

____

____

Unit 14 Tsunami Wiki

A singular subject needs a singular verb. A plural subject needs a plural verb. For example, *I am happy*, and, *We are happy*. We call this **subject–verb agreement**. A **statement** is a sentence that gives a fact or an opinion.

Explanation – Wiki

A wiki is a website that can be created and edited by more than one person.

Home | About | Contacts

Websites have tabs that help to organise information.

Tsunamis

What is a tsunami?

Introduction to the topic.

A tsunami is a giant wall of water made up of sets of huge waves. A tsunami can be up to 30 metres tall when it reaches land. Some tsunami waves can be 200 kilometres long.

The word “tsunami” is Japanese. It means “harbour wave”.

Series of explanations about the topic.

How do tsunamis occur?

Tsunamis occur when there is movement on the ocean floor. This can be from underwater earthquakes, landslides or volcanoes. When the sea floor moves, the sea level rises. Huge waves rush out from the centre of the movement. The waves become bigger and more powerful as they travel towards land.

1 **Draw a star next to each question in the wiki.**

2 **Read these sentences. Underline the questions in blue. Underline the statements in red.**

a What is a tsunami?

b A tsunami is a giant wall of water.

c How do tsunamis occur?

d Tsunamis occur when there is movement on the ocean floor.

3 **Complete these sentences using verbs from the box. Remember the subject and the verb need to agree.**

occur	moves	can	means

a The word tsunami ________________ "harbour wave" in Japanese.

b Tsunamis ________________ cause a lot of damage when they reach land.

c Tsunamis ________________ when there is movement on the ocean floor.

d When the sea floor ________________, the sea level rises.

4 **Draw a line to match the phrase with its correct ending to make a question or a statement.**

a Would you like	our favourite sport.
b I am going	railway station?
c Where is the	the pasta or the pizza?
d Basketball is	on holiday.

5 **Cross out the verb that does not agree with the subject in the questions.**

a What cause / causes thunder and lightning?

b What happen / happens to the waves in a tsunami?

c How do cyclones occur / occurs?

6 **Write an answer to each of these questions. Remember, your answer will be a statement that includes a subject and a verb.**

a What is your favourite sport?

____

b How many brothers and sisters do you have?

____

c Where do you and your family live?

____

7 **Rewrite these sentences by changing either the subject or the verb so they are correct. The first one has been done for you.**

a The babies drinks from her bottle.

The baby drinks from her bottle.

b Marcos and Siena walks to the shop.

____

c The car race around the track.

____

8 **Write an explanation about how something works or how something happens. Here are some topics you could write about.**

- All about glaciers
- Where do rainbows come from?
- Why some animals hibernate

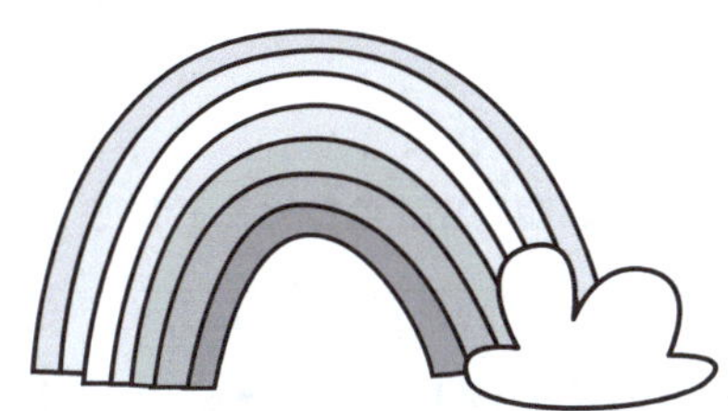

Wiki

Home | About | Contacts

Title	
Introduction	
Explanations	

Unit 15 Isaac's Interview

An **apostrophe** (') is a punctuation mark used to show ownership, for example *Mia's balloon*. The balloon belongs to Mia. Apostrophes can also be used to shorten a word. For example, *You're going to win the race!* You + are = you're. Words like this are called **contractions**.

Interview – Question and Answer

An interview is a conversation between at least two people, where one person asks questions for the other person to answer.

Isaac's Interview with Dylan Stockland

Introduction

Dylan Stockland is Isaac's favourite rugby league player. Isaac won a competition to interview Dylan for school. Here are some of Isaac's questions and Dylan's answers.

Apostrophe of ownership.

Questions and answers.

Isaac: What is your best achievement in rugby league?

Dylan: I've been part of a team that has won three premiership titles.

Isaac: What makes a great player?

Dylan: Great players play fair and are good sports. It's important to play together as a team.

Contraction

Isaac: What are some things we don't know about you?

Dylan: My nickname is Stocky and I kick with my left foot.

1 **Circle the apostrophes that are used to show ownership in the interview in red.**

2 **Circle the apostrophes that are used to shorten words in the interview in blue.**

3 **Add the missing apostrophes of ownership to these sentences.**

a Dylans birthday is 19 August.

b Dylans strength is his goal-kicking.

c Dylan is Isaacs favourite player.

d Dylans best score in a game is 12 points.

4 **Circle the apostrophes that are used to show ownership in these sentences in red. Circle the apostrophes that are used to shorten words in these sentences in blue.**

a You're very good at playing guitar.

b Sarah's dress is yellow.

c He's my favourite player.

d That soccer ball is Nick's.

5 **Write who or what is the owner of these things.**

a Tran's bike ______________________

b My mum's job ______________________

c The elephant's trunk ______________________

d The teacher's books ______________________

6 **Rewrite these sentences using shortened words. Remember to include apostrophes.**

a He is reading a book.

____

b We are going to the zoo.

____

c You are my hero.

____

7 **Rewrite these phrases using apostrophes that show ownership. The first one has been done for you.**

a The cow of the farmer

The farmer's cow

b The beak of the pelican

____

c The costume of the clown

____

8 **Write a sentence using a word with an apostrophe to match each picture. Remember, apostrophes can shorten a word or show ownership.**

a

____

b

c

9 Imagine you have interviewed your favourite sportsperson. Write your interview below.

Introduction	
Question	
Answer	
Question	
Answer	

Unit 16 Izzie's Treasure

Evaluative language uses words that express opinion or judgement about people or things. For example, *The film was so boring*. **Modal adverbs** add meaning to verbs by telling us how certain something is. For example, *My toe is probably broken.*

Review – Film Review

A film review uses words of judgement to give an opinion about a film.

Izzie's Treasure

A summary of the film.

Izzie's Treasure is an adventure film set in a small village. One day, Izzie sets out to solve an ancient family mystery. She must find a treasure box before the ink on her map fades away.

Evaluative language is used to praise the film.

Izzie's Treasure will probably win the best film of the year. From the very beginning you are caught up in a fascinating journey. This exciting film really keeps you guessing. *Izzie's Treasure* is clearly a fun film for children and those who are children at heart.

You must not miss *Izzie's Treasure*!

Final comment and recommendation for the film.

1 **Circle the modal adverbs in the review. Use the words in the box to help you.**

clearly probably really

2 **Underline the evaluative words in the review. Use the words in the box to help you.**

fascinating fun exciting

3 **Find these modal adverbs in the word search.**

HARDLY CLEARLY NEARLY PROBABLY REALLY

P	L	Y	L	R	A	E	N
A	R	F	J	Y	I	D	R
M	E	O	C	H	Q	F	H
W	A	E	B	G	C	E	A
B	L	I	J	A	X	K	R
T	L	G	O	V	B	D	D
N	Y	U	K	B	P	L	L
Y	L	R	A	E	L	C	Y

4 **Write a modal adverb in the spaces provided to complete these sentences.**

a We should ______________ unpack the car.

b He had ______________ made a mistake.

c If we run we will ______________ make it in time.

5 **Complete these sentences using the correct modal adverb from the box. The first one has been done for you.**

definitely	clearly	~~hardly~~	nearly	probably

a You could hardly blame him.

b It was ______________ sunset.

c We will ______________ see that film.

d They are ______________ in the wrong.

e This is ______________ a case for the detective.

6 **Write a sentence about these things using evaluative language.**

a a film ______________________________

b a book ______________________________

c a restaurant ______________________________

d a TV show ______________________________

7 **Write a sentence to match each picture. Use a verb and a modal adverb in each.**

a

____

b

____

c

____

8 **Rewrite these sentences by replacing the underlined evaluative words with different evaluative words.**

a This book is truly <u>interesting</u>.

____

b *Izzie's Treasure* is clearly a <u>fun</u> film.

____

c The football match was so <u>exciting</u>.

____

9 **Write your own film review for a film you have seen recently. Remember to use evaluative language and modal adverbs.**

Title	
Summary of film	
Evaluation	
Final comment	

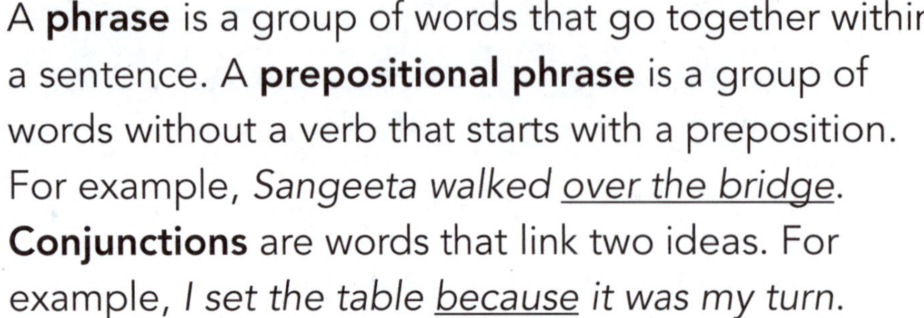

Unit 17 Farewell Party

A **phrase** is a group of words that go together within a sentence. A **prepositional phrase** is a group of words without a verb that starts with a preposition. For example, *Sangeeta walked* *over the bridge*. **Conjunctions** are words that link two ideas. For example, *I set the table* *because* *it was my turn*.

Transactional – Invitation

An invitation is a request to attend an event.

Lin and Mei's Farewell Party

Greeting

Dear Erin,

The Yins are moving across Australia.
We want more warm weather because we are cold!
Don't cry yet! Please come over to our place for a sleepover farewell party before we leave.

Details of the party, including when it will take place, where, and what to wear.

Date: Saturday 12 May at 7:00 pm

Theme: Fancy dress

Place: 14 Frangipani Lane, Partyville, 1000

Please bring your pyjamas, a set of spare clothes, and a photo of yourself for us to keep.

RSVP: Please contact Lin or Mei so we know how much popcorn to make.

So is a conjunction.

Sender details

From Lin and Mei ♡

1 **Circle three different conjunctions in the invitation. Use the words in the box to help you.**

and so or because

2 **Underline three prepositional phrases in the invitation. The first one has been done for you.**

3 **Find these conjunctions in the word search.**

AND	OR
WHILE	BUT
BECAUSE	THOUGH
SO	FOR
YET	

O	Z	A	H	B	P	E
R	W	N	G	N	S	O
A	H	D	T	U	M	I
R	I	Q	A	Y	J	U
S	L	C	U	E	C	R
B	E	F	E	T	V	O
B	U	T	L	D	W	F
T	H	O	U	G	H	X

4 **Circle the conjunctions in these sentences.**

a I enjoyed the book, but it could have been better.

b We can play basketball or we can go for a bike ride.

c The athletics event was cancelled because it was raining.

d The party was fancy dress and everyone was excited.

5 **Complete each sentence with a prepositional phrase that tells *where*. The first one has been done for you.**

a The bear slept in a dark cave ______________________.

b My dad runs ______________________.

c Grandad meets his friends ______________________.

d Tasmanian devils live ______________________.

e Let's go for a picnic ______________________.

6 **Complete these sentences using conjunctions from the box.**

and   but   so   or   because

a We are saving our money ____________ we can buy new shoes.

b Sleepover parties are fun ____________ you don't get much sleep.

c I am not allowed to go to Sari's ____________ I didn't finish my homework.

d Please bring some games ____________ your bike.

e Would you like the apple ____________ the orange?

7 **Complete each sentence with a prepositional phrase that tells *why*.**

a I would like to go but I'm busy that day ______________________.

b He put on his coat ______________________.

c Elise wanted new shoes ______________________.

d The tiger roared loudly ______________________.

8 **Complete each sentence with a prepositional phrase that tells *when*.**

a We'll go back to school after the summer holidays.

b Dinner starts ______________________________.

c My birthday party ______________________________.

9 **Create your own invitation for a party. Remember to include a few conjunctions you have learned today.**

Dear ______________________________

____

____

____

Date: ______________________________

Theme: ______________________________

Place: ______________________________

RSVP: ______________________________

From: ______________________________

10 **The Yins are moving to Brisbane. Find Brisbane on an online map.**

Unit 18 The Missing Diary

A **pronoun** is a word that takes the place of a noun. For example, instead of saying, *<u>Eric</u> dressed up as a pirate*, we can say, *<u>He</u> dressed up as a pirate*. Pronouns can also replace a thing or things using *it*, or *they*. **Rhythm** is created in poems or stories by repeating or stressing certain words or syllables – the small parts of a word.

Narrative – Story

A narrative is a story that tells events and entertains.

The Missing Diary

The introduction sets the scene and introduces the characters.

Amy loved to write in her diary. Each day, she wrote about her secrets and what was happening in her life.

Amy's brother was having a party in the tree house in the backyard. He dressed up as a pirate.

The events leading to a problem.

After the party, Amy snuck up to her room. She looked for her diary under her pillow. It wasn't there. She looked for her diary under the bed. It wasn't there. She looked on her book shelf. It wasn't there!

Rhythm is created by repeating words or phrases.

Amy retraced her steps to the tree house in the backyard. There it was! Her diary was hidden under some streamers and wrapping paper.

The story's resolution.

Amy was very relieved.

1 **Circle the *he, she* and *it* pronouns in the story.**

2 **Underline the repeated phrases that create rhythm in the story.**

3 **Draw a line to match the name or names to the correct pronoun.**

a Goldilocks — he

b Prince Charming — they

c Jack and Jill — she

4 **Complete these sentences by replacing the name or names with the pronoun *she* or *they*.**

a Amy loved to write in her diary.

______________ loved to write in her diary.

b Amy was getting worried.

______________ was getting worried.

c Mum and Grace look alike, don't you think?

______________ look alike, don't you think?

5 **Use the pronoun *it* or *they* to complete these sentences.**

a Amy looked under her bed for her diary, but ______________ wasn't there.

b Chen and Robert were bored, so ______________ played video games for an hour.

c I had extra cake, so I shared ______________ with James.

d Alison and Miguel love running and ______________ are good at ______________.

6 Replace the underlined names with pronouns.

a <u>Tamara</u> went to the zoo.

_____________ went to the zoo.

b <u>Mason</u> rode the roller-coaster.

_____________ rode the roller-coaster.

c <u>Dad and I</u> gave the gift to Eve.

_____________ gave the gift to Eve.

d <u>Ada and Leah</u> are sisters.

_____________ are sisters.

7 Complete these sentences with pronouns.

a _____________ walked to school.

b _____________ are going to the fun park.

c _____________ is so much taller than me.

d Victor and Emma were the first ones to notice _____________ in the tree.

8 Read the story below. Underline the repeated words that help to create rhythm.

Billy had always wanted a skateboard. He had wanted a skateboard since his last birthday. He wanted a skateboard so much that he decided to start a paper run to make money to buy a skateboard. When Billy bought the skateboard he fell off it and broke his wrist. Billy has now decided to save up for something less dangerous.

9 **Rewrite these sentences using pronouns.**

a Fatima washed her feet before Fatima went to bed.

____

b Josh used his dad's hammer without asking first.

____

c You and I are going to Casie's birthday party.

____

10 **Write your own short story. Remember to include pronouns.**

Title	
Introduction	
Events and a problem	
Resolution	

Unit 19 Come to Uluru!

A **statement of fact** is a sentence that is true. A **modal verb** is a verb that tells us how likely or necessary something is. Modal verbs can be high in modality (*will*, *must*, *should*) or low in modality (*might*, *may*, *could*).

Persuasive – Brochure

A persuasive text wants you to do or think something.

Come to Uluru!

Introduction

Uluru is the best natural landmark in Australia. You must see it. You will have an amazing experience.

Statements of fact about Uluru.

Uluru is a rock formation that is 500 million years old, and is about 346 metres high.

A series of arguments.

You should visit this sacred Aboriginal site. You will learn that its traditional owners are the Anangu people.

You cannot miss seeing Uluru at sunrise and sunset. You will be amazed at how it changes colour dramatically. You may never want to go home!

The conclusion encourages the reader to visit Uluru.

Uluru has many outstanding features. It should definitely be on your holiday list.

1 **Underline two statements of fact about Uluru in the brochure.**

2 **Circle the modal verbs in the brochure. Use the words in the box to help you.**

must	should	cannot	will	may

3 **Unscramble these modal verbs. Write the correct spellings in the spaces provided.**

a oushld ____________

b yam ____________

c stum ____________

d ghtmi ____________

e llwi ____________

f cloud ____________

4 **Complete these sentences using the modal verbs from the box.**

should	must	may	will

a You ____________ be amazed at how it changes colour.

b You ____________ see it in your lifetime.

c You ____________ never want to go home.

d You ____________ tell your friends all about it!

5 **Tick the sentence of each pair that is a statement of fact.**

a Uluru is 500 million years old.
You should visit this sacred site.

b The traditional owners of Uluru are the Anangu people.
You may never want to go home.

6 Circle the modal verbs in these sentences.

a She should eat her vegetables.

b The new puppy may arrive tonight.

c They must hurry or they will miss the train.

7 Rewrite the sentences in the table using verbs that are high in modality. The first one has been done for you.

Low modal verbs	High modal verbs
You could wash your face every day.	You should wash your face every day.
You may have lollies after your dinner.	
He might tidy his room.	

8 Write a statement of fact to match each picture.

a ______________________________

b ______________________________

Pineapples

c ______________________________

9 **Replace the underlined low modal verbs in these sentences with high modal verbs.**

a You <u>might</u> want to go on a holiday.

____

b I <u>could</u> help out at the school fair.

____

c He <u>may</u> be able to come to the movies.

____

10 **Write a travel brochure about your perfect place to go on holiday. Remember to use modal verbs to persuade others to visit!**

Title	
Introduction	
Series of arguments	
Conclusion	

Unit 20 Bird Life

Onomatopoeia describes a word that imitates its sound, for example *boom* and *crunch*. **Rhythmic patterns** are created by repeating or stressing certain words or syllables – the small parts of a word. Rhythmic patterns sound like beats in a line of poetry. For example, *Twinkle, twinkle, little star*. The underlined syllables show the beats.

Description – Poem

A description describes the features of something.

Title of the poem.

Onomatopoeia is used for the words *crunching* and *swooshing*.

Sounds are repeated for rhythm.

Bird Life

Crunching, swooshing, hip hooray,
Gathering leaves for my nest today.

Rustling, rattling, what a catch,
A nice and juicy earthworm patch.

Tooting, tweeting, from my beak,
Flapping wings and scuttling feet.

Splashing, sploshing, what a hoot,
Toe of frog and eye of newt.

Whooshing, whizzing, over trees,
So high up and flying free!

1 **Underline the onomatopoeic words in the poem beginning with the letter *s*. Use the words in the box to help you.**

swooshing	sploshing	splashing

2 **Circle the onomatopoeic words in the poem beginning with the letter *w*. Use the words in the box to help you.**

whizzing	whooshing

3 **Draw a star near all the remaining onomatopoeic words you can find in the poem.**

4 **Underline the beats that are stressed in the poem below. The first line has been done for you.**

<u>Twin</u>kle, <u>twin</u>kle, <u>lit</u>tle <u>star</u>,
How I wonder what you are.
Up above the world so high,
Like a diamond in the sky.

5 **Circle four onomatopoeic words in the list below.**

watch	boom	cry	woof
achoo	simple	ouch	kite

6 **Draw a line to match the onomatopoeic word to its relating noun.**

a banging — bubbles
b ticking — drum
c booming — clock
d popping — thunder

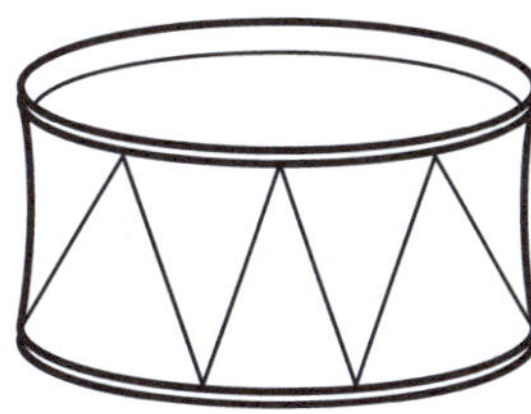

7 **Underline the syllables in the words that show rhythmic pattern. The first one has been done for you.**

a Crunching, swooshing, hip hooray,
Gathering leaves for my nest today.

b Rustling, rattling, what a catch,
A nice and juicy earthworm patch.

8 **Unscramble the letters to make onomatopoeic words.**

a laspsh! ____________________

b ppo! ____________________

c ueasqk! ____________________

d hiwzz! ____________________

9 **Write an onomatopoeic word beginning with the letters below. The first one has been done for you.**

Letter	Onomatopoeic word
s	sizzle
b	
w	

10 **Write an onomatopoeic word to describe each noun.**

a cat ____________________

b fire ____________________

c duck ____________________

11 **Use these onomatopoeic words in a short paragraph.**

bang   crash   crack

12 **Write your own poem including onomatopoeic words. Here are some topics you could write about.**

- A baby crying
- A motor car race
- Animals on a farm

Unit 21 Thai Greetings

A **statement of opinion** is someone's view or judgement about something. A **contraction** is made by joining two words to make one shorter word. Contractions use an apostrophe ('). For example, *I will*, becomes *I'll*.

Recount – Postcard

Dear Grandad is the greeting used to start the postcard.

I've is the contraction of *I have*.

Name and address of person receiving the postcard.

Dear Grandad,

Greetings from Thailand! We've had a great time on our holiday so far. You wouldn't believe how hot it is here. I've been swimming at the beach every day. It's very beautiful.

Yesterday we went to an elephant park. I didn't get to ride one though. I'm a bit sad about that.

We've visited many small villages and met many nice people.

You'll have to come with us next time. See you soon!

Love from Mali xx

This is the writer's personal opinion.

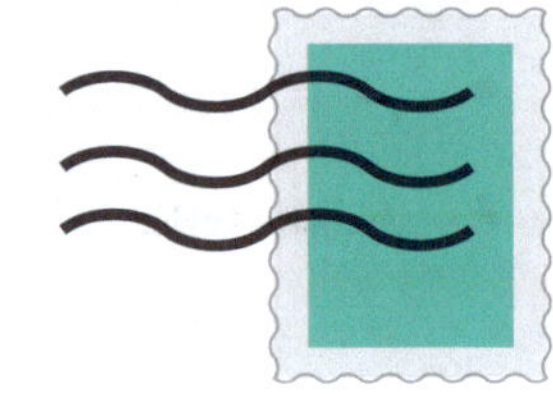

Adam Malouf
25 Stanford Rd
Packsville
Queensland 4567

1 **Circle the contractions in the postcard. Use the words in the box to help you.**

didn't wouldn't I'm I've you'll we've it's

2 **Write two statements from the postcard that give Mali's opinion of her holiday.**

____

____

3 **Write apostrophes in the correct places in these contractions.**

a I m
d w o n t
e s h e l l
b w e v e
c c a n t
f d i d n t

4 **Match the words to the contractions.**

a I am	She's
b She is	He'll
c He will	I'm
d They will	They'll

5 **Draw a smiley face next to the positive opinions and a sad face next to the negative opinions in these sentences.**

a I had lots of fun watching the football game last week.

b The noisy group ruined our day.

c It was a really great party.

d That film is not funny.

6 **Rewrite these sentences using contractions.**

a I did not want to go to school.

____

b We will not be coming over today.

____

c She could not reach the top shelf.

____

d You have got nice eyes.

____

7 **Tick the statements of opinion. Draw a star next to the statements of fact. Remember, a statement of fact is a sentence that is true.**

a The cat licked its milk from the bowl.
A cat is the best pet in the world.

b I wouldn't like to meet a lion in the wild.
Lions roam in the wild, searching for food.

c Everybody should be collecting grey water.
We collect grey water to water our garden.

d There are 52 cards in a deck of playing cards.
My grandmother is good at playing card games.

8 **Write a sentence to give your opinion about these topics.**

a Horror films

____

b Australian Rules football

____

c Rock music

____

9 **Write a postcard to a friend from the Gold Coast. Include your personal opinion about the things you see and use some contractions. Find the Gold Coast on an online map.**

To

Unit 22

Balloon Rockets

A **conditional sentence** uses words such as *would* and *if* to describe something that might happen. They refer to imaginary or **hypothetical situations**. For example, *I would go if I was feeling better.* A **present tense verb** tells us about an action that is happening now or that happens regularly.

Procedure – Experiment

A procedure instructs how to make or do something.

How to make a balloon rocket

You will need:

- a drinking straw
- a piece of string
- 2 strong tables
- a balloon
- a paperclip
- sticky tape

What to do:

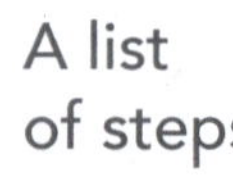

Present tense verbs.

1. Thread the drinking straw onto a piece of string.
2. Tie one end of the string to a table leg. Tie the other end of the string to a leg on the other table. Keep the string tight.
3. Blow up the balloon and hold its neck together with a paperclip.
4. Tape the balloon to the straw.
5. Push the straw and balloon to one end of the string.
6. Take the paperclip off the balloon and watch your rocket take off.

These are hypothetical questions.

Think about ...

What would happen if you changed something in this experiment?

What would happen if the balloon wasn't blown up completely?

1 **Underline the present tense verbs in the experiment. The first one has been done for you.**

2 **Tick the conditional sentences in the experiment.**

3 **Replace the underlined present tense verbs so that these instructions make sense. The first one has been done for you.**

a Thread the balloon to the straw.

Tape the balloon to the straw.

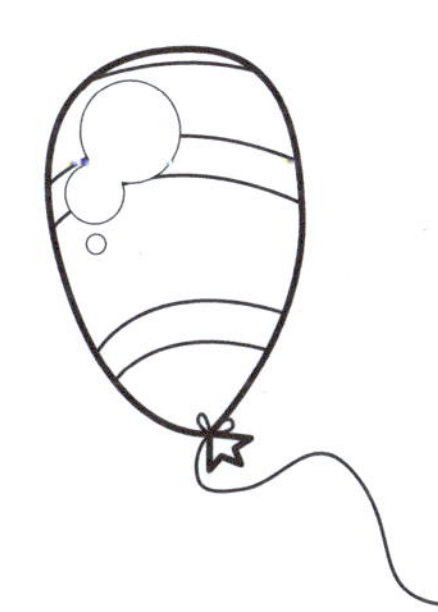

b Inflate the straw and balloon to one end of the string.

____

c Blow up the paperclip off the balloon.

____

d Run the string tight.

____

4 **Circle the present tense verbs in the pairs below.**

a buy / bought

b caught / catch

c attach / attached

d pulled / pull

e laughed / laugh

f run / ran

5 **Complete these conditional sentences using words from the box. You will need to use some words more than once.**

if would will

a ______________ you come to my house, we can watch TV.

b Tom ______________ pick you up in his car ______________ he has time.

c Laura ______________ go to the concert ______________ she had tickets.

d We ______________ walk to school ______________ the weather was nicer.

6 **Tick the conditional sentences.**

a If the fire went out, we would get very cold.

b We will shine our torches in the dark.

c You will be sorry if you don't come home soon.

d If you don't study, you won't know the answer.

e Poke a hole in the middle of the cardboard.

7 **Complete these sentences with present tense verbs.**

a ______________ the water into a bowl.

b ______________ in an oven for ten minutes.

c ______________ the paper into thin strips.

d ______________ the napkin in half.

8 **Draw a line to match the conditional sentence opening to its correct ending.**

a I would help	if you were in my shoes?
b What would you do	we could have gone to the beach.
c If the weather was sunny	if I could.
d He would play soccer	if she hears a knock.
e She'll answer the door	if he could find his boots.

9 **Write a conditional sentence using each pair of words. The first one has been done for you.**

a quiet / kangaroo

If you're really quiet, you might see a kangaroo!

b coat / snow

c exercise / fit

d practice / win

Unit 23
Down by the Sea

An **idiom** is a saying that has a hidden meaning. For example, if something is easy, it is *a piece of cake*. Verbs that show emotion are called **feeling verbs**. For example, *I hate the rain.* Song lyrics often use idioms and **emotive language** to express meaning and emotion.

Description – Song Lyrics

Song lyrics are words in a song.

Down by the Sea

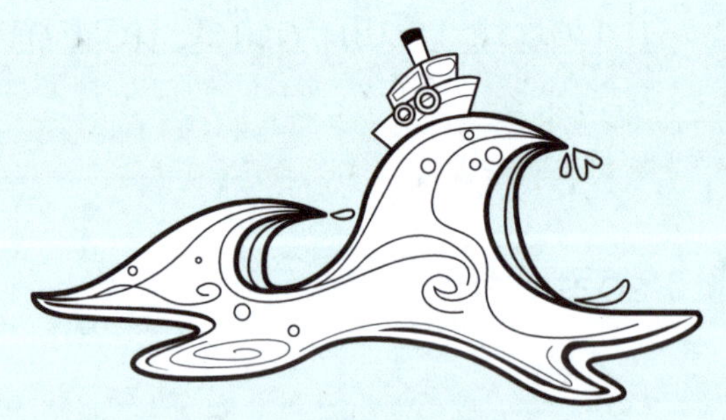

The ocean calls me softly,
I love its bouncing waves.
A seagull spots some fish,
That escape to secret caves.

Sentences in song lyrics are called lines.

You are the sun in my sky,
The apple of my eye.
Sea sounds are music to my ears,
I hate to say goodbye.

This song lyric uses idioms to describe things in an imaginative way.

A group of lines in a song lyric is called a verse.

1 **Underline the idioms in the song lyrics. Use the words in the box to help you.**

music to my ears	sun in my sky	apple of my eye

2 **Circle the feeling verbs *love* and *hate* in the song lyrics.**

3 **Find these feeling verbs in the word search.**

LOVE	DISAPPOINT	EXCITED	WORRY
UPSET	LIKE	ENJOY	SCARED

E	J	Q	D	H	U	P	S	E	T
T	N	I	O	P	P	A	S	I	D
I	E	R	I	E	V	O	L	S	P
L	N	X	Q	T	D	B	X	C	F
D	J	M	C	P	E	K	T	A	Y
T	O	Y	Z	I	R	D	O	R	R
K	Y	S	W	L	T	C	F	E	R
P	I	Z	U	G	E	E	A	D	O
D	V	H	E	K	I	L	D	P	W

4 **Draw a smiley face next to the sentences that are idioms.**

a We're all in the same boat.

b The ocean is deep.

c I'll go out on a limb.

d It's the icing on the cake.

e The trees are tall.

f Today is my birthday.

5 **Circle the feeling verbs in the list below.**

run	excite	love	fly
ski	hate	write	proud

6 **Draw a line to match the idiom to its meaning.**

a start from scratch — to get married

b tie the knot — ask someone to listen to you

c lend me your ear — to begin all over again

d monkey business — cheeky behaviour

7 **Match the idiom on the left to a picture on the right.**

a Jumping for joy

b The foot of the mountain

c The heart of a lion

8 **Write a sentence with an emotive verb to describe each picture.**

a

____

b

____

c

d

9 **Write song lyrics of your own. Try to include at least two idioms you have learned today. Here are some topics you could write about.**

- Dancing to the beat
- An unbelievable day
- Being lost in space

Title: ______________________________

Unit 24 The Moon Landing

A **compound sentence** contains two clauses, usually joined with a conjunction and sometimes a comma. **Relating verbs** show the relationship that exists between two things. Relating verbs are either part of the verb *to be* (*am*, *are*, *is*, *was*, *were*) or the verb *to have* (*have*, *has*, *had*).

Recount – Historical

A historical recount retells events from the past.

The Moon Landing

The introduction summarises the event and the people involved.

Apollo 11 was the name of the space flight that transported the first humans to the Moon. Neil Armstrong, Edwin 'Buzz' Aldrin and Michael Collins were the astronauts on board the spacecraft.

Events are explained in order of when they happened.

On 20 July 1969, Armstrong became the first person to walk on the Moon. The world watched on television as he climbed down the ladder of *Apollo 11* and onto the surface of the Moon. Aldrin also walked on the Moon, while Collins stayed in the command ship.

This compound sentence is joined by a comma and the conjunction *while*.

Summary and final comment about the event.

It was a great achievement to land a human on the moon, and it is a historical event that will not be forgotten.

1 **Circle the relating verbs in the recount.**

2 **Find these relating verbs in the word search.**

HAD IS WERE HAVE ARE BE HAS WAS AM

E	J	I	M	O	W	S
R	K	S	N	P	A	R
B	E	V	A	H	R	T
I	R	P	F	S	E	G
A	E	L	A	O	A	H
M	W	D	A	H	N	W

3 **Underline the compound sentences below. Circle the conjunctions in each compound sentence.**

a The bee made honey.

b The waves became bigger when the wind blew stronger.

c The bus drove down the bumpy road and got a flat tyre.

d The girl rang the bell.

4 **Draw a line down to match the verb to its relating verb variations.**

to have **to be**

was had were are is has am

5 Complete these compound sentences using conjunctions from the box.

when and because or but

a I wanted to go, ____________ I wasn't allowed.

b The wizard waved his wand ____________ cast a spell.

c The ground dried up ____________ the sun came out.

d The cats hissed ____________ there was a bird in the tree.

e You must go to school ____________ I will take you to the doctor.

6 Rewrite each pair of simple sentences into one compound sentence with a conjunction.

a He was small. He was strong.

____

b We gobbled up the cake. We gobbled up the biscuits.

____

c The dog barked. Someone banged on the door.

____

d The girl won the trophy. She trained very hard.

____

e The hiker was tired. She kept climbing.

____

7 **Write a sentence using each relating verb.**

a am

____

b are

____

8 **Write a recount about a past event. Use compound sentences and relating verbs. Here are some topics you could write about.**

- The first Anzac Day
- A family's arrival in Australia
- The story of Federation

Title	
Introduction	
Events in the correct order	
Final comment	

Unit 25 What's a Website?

A **paragraph** is a sentence or group of sentences based on the same idea. A paragraph begins on a new line. A **comparative adjective** is a type of adjective used to compare two things. A **superlative adjective** compares more than two things. For example, *Emma is a* *faster* (comparative) *runner than Indira, but Kate is the* *fastest* (superlative).

Explanation – Website

A website is a group of pages on the World Wide Web.

www.websites.com

Home | **About** | **Contacts**

How a Website Works

Websites use the internet to share information with people all over the world. Websites have text, pictures and links to other pages and websites.

Computer language can be used to tell the computer to make text and pictures bigger or smaller.

To access websites you need a computer and a connection to the internet. A web address usually starts with the letters www.

The simplest website can be one page. The largest website can have an infinite number of pages.

All websites link together to make the World Wide Web.

Introduction and general statement.

These paragraphs explain how websites work.

Superlative adjectives.

Conclusion or summary.

1 **Draw a star at the beginning of each new paragraph in the website.**

2 **Circle the comparative and superlative adjectives in the website. Use the words in the box to help you.**

smaller bigger largest simplest

3 **Write a comparative and superlative adjective for the words in the table. The first one has been done for you.**

Adjective	Comparative	Superlative
big	bigger	biggest
small		
long		
easy		

4 **Draw a star where you think a new paragraph should begin.**

Honey is sticky and delicious. It gives you lots of energy and is better for you than sugar. Bees make honey. Bees have special jobs. Worker bees make honey from beeswax in their stomachs.

5 **Complete these sentences using comparative and superlative adjectives. The first one has been done for you.**

a A car is smaller than a bus, but a bicycle is smallest of all.

b ______________ is bigger than ______________, but ______________ is biggest of all.

c ______________ is quieter than ______________, but ______________ is quietest of all.

6 **Sort these sentences into topics to make three different paragraphs of information. Write your paragraphs in the spaces below.**

Katia loves animals.

He took his racket with him.

Her mum bought her two goldfish.

Year 3 ate all the hot dogs.

Alex went to tennis practice.

They were so full they couldn't move.

a Food

____

____

b Animals

____

____

c Hobbies

____

____

7 **Write the correct comparative or superlative adjective to replace each adjective in brackets. The first one has been done for you.**

a The rainwater tank is much (full) fuller than it was last week.

b It is (hot) ____________ this summer than it was last year.

c Max looks (sad) ____________ than I have seen him in ages.

d It is (easy) ____________ to take Main Street.

8 **Write an explanation about how something works or how something happens. Remember to include superlative and comparative adjectives. Here are some topics you could write about.**

- How fish swim
- How volcanoes erupt
- How birds fly

Title	
Introduction	
A number of statements to explain *how*	
Conclusion or summary	

Glossary

action verb	a word that expresses doing or being
adjective	a word that describes a noun
adverb	a word that tells us more about a verb
apostrophe	a punctuation mark (') used to show ownership or to shorten a word
article	a word used to refer to a noun (e.g. a, an, the)
capital letter	a letter used at the start of a sentence
clause	a group of related words containing a subject and a verb
comma	a punctuation mark (,) used to separate thoughts and ideas
command	a sentence that tells someone to do something
comparative adjective	a type of adjective used to compare two things
compound sentence	a sentence made up of two simple sentences
conditional sentence	a sentence that describes something that might happen
conjunction	a word used to link two ideas (e.g. and, but, so)
contraction	two words joined to make one shorter word using an apostrophe (e.g. I'll, they're)
emotive language	words that try to make us feel something
evaluative language	words that express opinion or judgement about people or things
exclamation mark	a punctuation mark (!) used to give emphasis or show surprise, shock or joy
full stop	a punctuation mark (.) used to show the end of a sentence
idiom	a saying that has a hidden meaning
modal adjective	a type of adjective used to show how possible or necessary something is (e.g. definite, probable, usual)
modal adverb	a type of adverb used to show how possible or certain something is (e.g. definitely, probably, maybe)
modal verb	a type of verb used to show how likely or necessary something is (e.g. will, may, should)
noun	a word that names people, places and things
noun group	a noun and a group of words that tells us more about the noun
onomatopoeia	when a word imitates its sound
paragraph	one or more sentences based on the same topic
past tense verb	a word that tells us actions that happened in the past
phrase	a group of words that go together within a sentence
precise language	language that uses words that are clear and to the point

preposition	a word that shows the relationship of a noun to another word (e.g. under, over, across)
prepositional phrase	a group of words without a verb that starts with a preposition
pronoun	a word that takes the place of a noun (e.g. I, you, we)
relating verb	a verb that shows the relationship between ideas in a clause
rhythm	a pattern of stressed words or syllables
saying verb	a verb used to show speech; often used instead of the word "said"
simple sentence	a group of words that contains a subject and a verb
statement of fact	a sentence that gives true information about something
statement of opinion	a sentence that shows someone's view or judgement
superlative adjective	a type of adjective used to compare more than two things
technical language	language that is special to science, art or a particular profession
technical noun	a noun used in technical language
verb	an action word that shows what is being done

This is to certify that

....

is a Grammar Guru

Signed ....

School ....

Date ....

GRAMMAR GURU